Before They Were Famous

Louisa May Alcott

Written by Stephen Krensky
Illustrated by Bobbie Houser

A Crabtree Crown Book

Crabtree Publishing
crabtreebooks.com

School-to-Home Support for Caregivers and Teachers

This book is designed to teach and appeal to a student on core subject areas. The student will build upon what they already know about the subject and engage in topics that they do not know but want to learn more about. Here are a few guiding questions to help the reader on his or her comprehension skills. Possible answers appear here in red.

Before Reading:

What do I know about this topic?

- *I know that Louisa May Alcott wrote the book Little Women.*
- *I know that when Louisa was growing up she had three sisters.*

What do I want to learn about this topic?

- *I want to learn more about Louisa's relationship with her sisters.*
- *I want to learn the titles of the other books Louisa May Alcott wrote.*

During Reading:

I'm curious to know...

- *I'm curious to know how Louisa got her first book published.*
- *I'm curious to know if Louisa's sisters were happy or angry that she was writing about their lives.*

How is this like something I already know?

- *I know that it's very difficult to get a book published.*
- *I know that sometimes sisters are jealous when one of them gets recognition for doing something special.*

After Reading:

What was the author trying to teach me?

- *I think the author was trying to teach me that you must have perseverance and never quit when you have a dream for yourself to achieve great things.*
- *I think the author was trying to teach me that although you may come from a poor family you can achieve great things in life.*

How did the photographs and captions help me understand more?

- *I didn't know that Louisa May Alcott was first published as a writer at age nineteen.*
- *I didn't know that Louisa became a nurse during the Civil War.*

Table of Contents

Wishing for More

Louisa Alcott was tired. How could she not be? She might feel all grown up at eighteen, but even so she was worn out from having one job after another. Already, she had worked as a **governess**, a **seamstress**, and a teacher. She could make floors shine and make dirty clothes clean and fresh.

But none of that was enough for her.

"I will do something, by and by," the young Louisa had declared. "Don't care what, teach, sew, act, write, anything to help the family; and I'll be rich and famous and happy before I die, see if I won't."

Fun Facts

Louisa's mother insisted that all her daughters have skills that would allow them to earn their own livings if necessary.

Louisa's mom

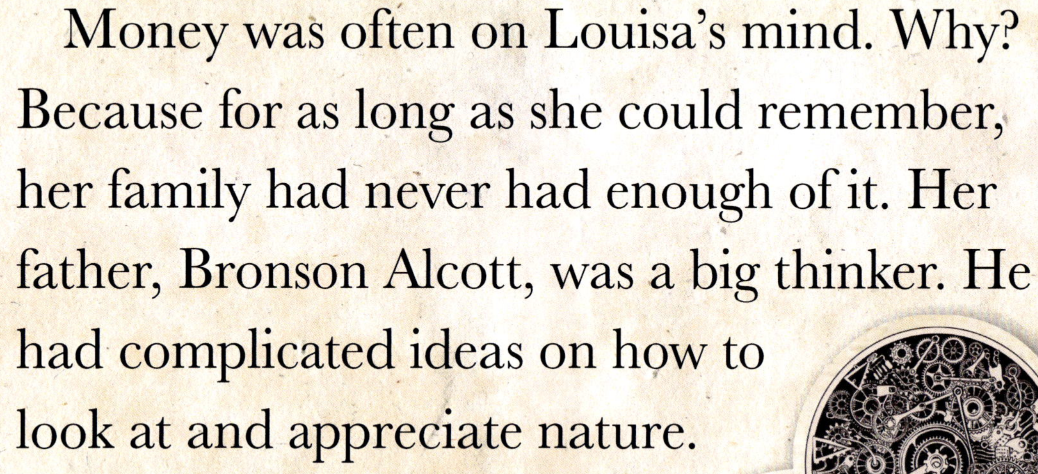

Money was often on Louisa's mind. Why? Because for as long as she could remember, her family had never had enough of it. Her father, Bronson Alcott, was a big thinker. He had complicated ideas on how to look at and appreciate nature.

Bronson Alcott

Fun Facts

Bronson Alcott changed his last name from Alcox and dropped his first name, Amos, entirely when he was a young man.

But these ideas did not help put food on his family's table. The Alcotts were poor, and Bronson's wife Abigail and their four daughters — Anna, Louisa, Elizabeth, and May — often went hungry.

Growing Up

To make matters worse, Louisa and her father were very different. Throughout her childhood, Louisa was an **unbridled** force. She saw herself as **spirited**, but her father saw her as troubled. Bronson liked nothing better than to sit for hours reading, writing, and thinking deep thoughts.

Fun Facts

Despite his very strong ideas about education, Bronson Alcott had spent very little time in school himself.

Not Louisa. She was always on the move. She liked to run and jump and dance whenever possible.

One thing Bronson Alcott did do, though, was give all his girls an education at home. This was unusual. In the 1840s, few American girls went to any kind of school. They were expected to grow up, get married, run a household, and fill it with children.

But for the Alcott girls, every day began with serious discussions over breakfast. These were followed by periods of study with reading, writing, and mathematics. More serious talk continued at lunch. Then the rest of the day was filled making art drawings or taking long walks.

Home Schooling

Fun Facts

One fun game Louisa and her sisters enjoyed was pushing a large rolling hoop with a stick.

On the Move

In 1840, when Louisa was 7 years old, her family moved from Boston to Concord, Massachusetts. It was a big change, but a happy one. Among their neighbors were some famous writers, including the philosopher Ralph Waldo Emerson and the **naturalist** Henry David Thoreau.

Ralph Waldo Emerson

Henry David Thoreau

Fun Facts

Henry David Thoreau gave lessons to Louisa about a decade before his famous book *Walden* was published.

BEST TEACHER EVER

Concord is 20 miles (32 km) west of Boston.

One of Bronson's ideas about how to better exist with nature led him to move his family again in 1843. This new and unusual community was a few miles from Concord. It was called Fruitlands.

Life in Fruitlands was harsh. Everyone had to get up before dawn, and there was only cold water for bathing. No animal products were eaten. That meant no meat, but also no eggs or cheese or milk. When winter came, the leaders even decided not to burn wood for warmth. It would be healthier, they thought, if everyone would just get used to being cold.

100% VEGAN

Fun Facts

Bronson Alcott's partner in creating Fruitlands was the philosopher, Charles Lane, who was even stricter than Bronson.

That was too much for Louisa's mother, Abigail. She convinced Bronson that Fruitlands was not a healthy place to raise their girls. And so, the Alcotts returned to Concord.

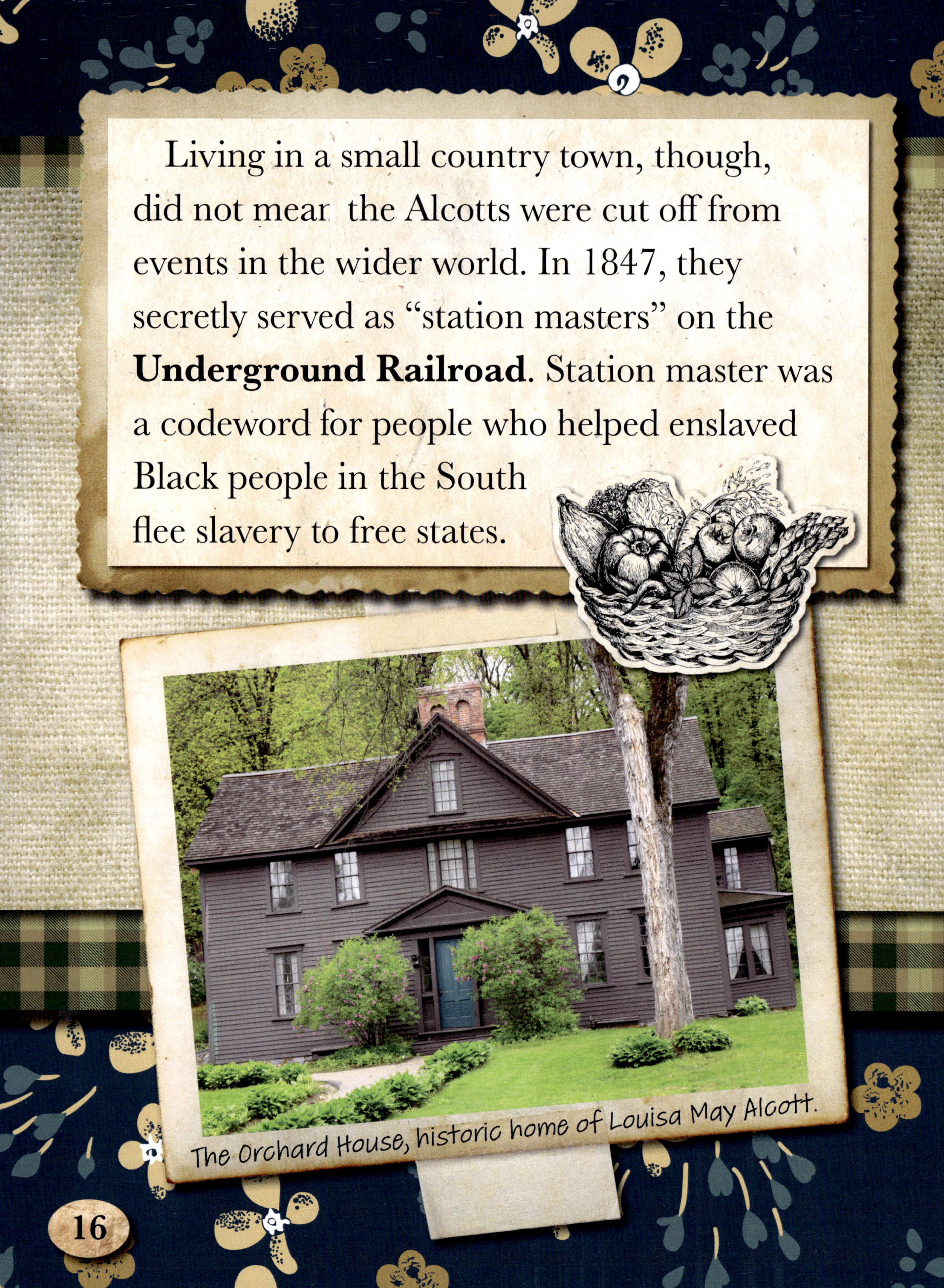

Living in a small country town, though, did not mear the Alcotts were cut off from events in the wider world. In 1847, they secretly served as "station masters" on the **Underground Railroad**. Station master was a codeword for people who helped enslaved Black people in the South flee slavery to free states.

The Orchard House, historic home of Louisa May Alcott.

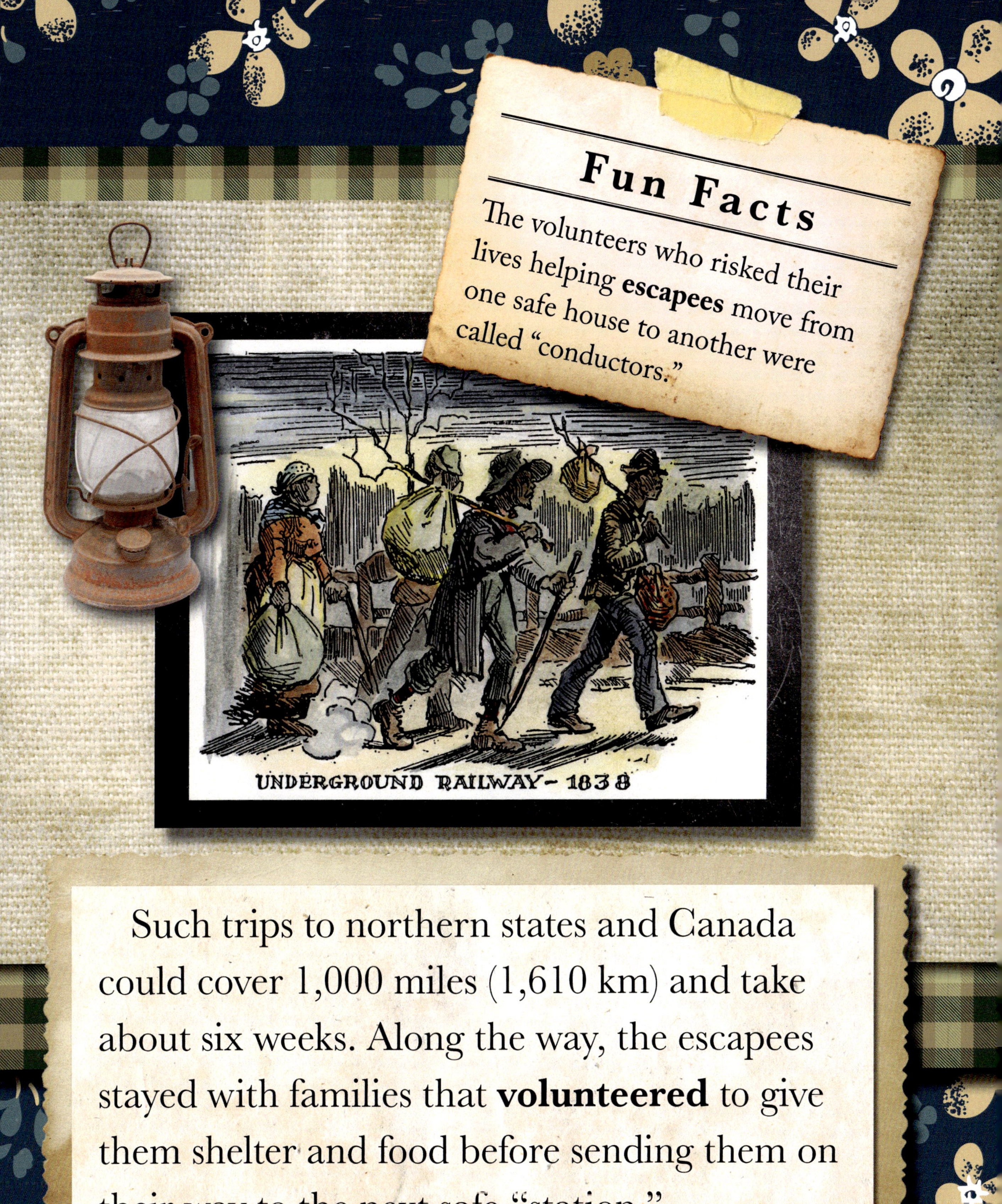

Fun Facts

The volunteers who risked their lives helping **escapees** move from one safe house to another were called "conductors."

Such trips to northern states and Canada could cover 1,000 miles (1,610 km) and take about six weeks. Along the way, the escapees stayed with families that **volunteered** to give them shelter and food before sending them on their way to the next safe "station."

Next Steps

In search of another job, Louisa now turned her attention to teaching her young neighbors, the Emerson girls. One of them, Ellen, loved to listen to Louisa make up stories, especially ones about magical creatures like elves and fairies.

Fun Facts

Louisa was first published as a writer at age nineteen when a poem of hers appeared in a magazine. However, she used a pen name, Flora Fairfield, rather than her real name.

Louisa wrote her stories down in a little book, which was published a few years later in 1854 as *Flower Fables*.

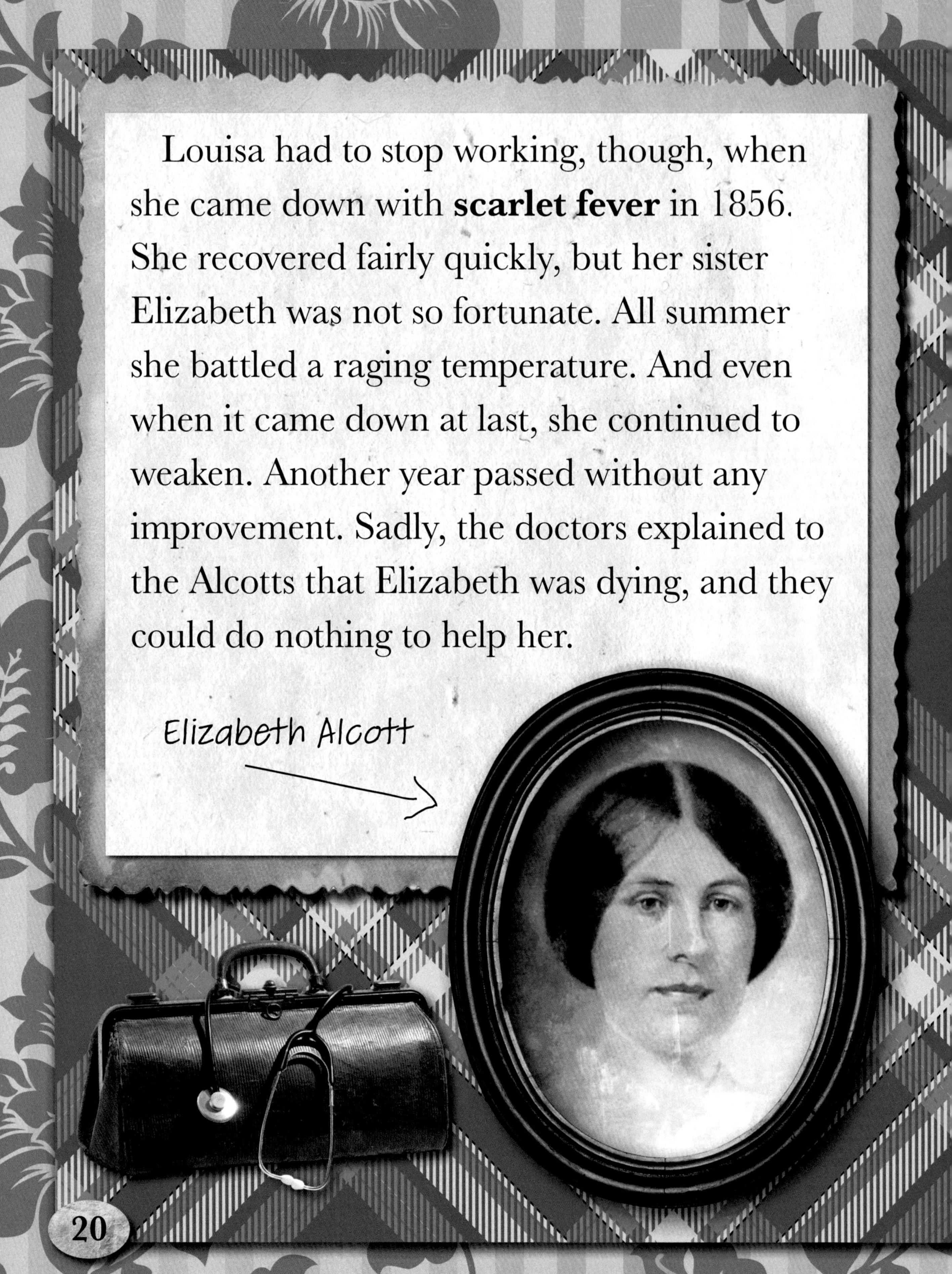

Louisa had to stop working, though, when she came down with **scarlet fever** in 1856. She recovered fairly quickly, but her sister Elizabeth was not so fortunate. All summer she battled a raging temperature. And even when it came down at last, she continued to weaken. Another year passed without any improvement. Sadly, the doctors explained to the Alcotts that Elizabeth was dying, and they could do nothing to help her.

Elizabeth Alcott

With Louisa at her side, Elizabeth passed away in March 1858.

Fun Facts

The character Beth March in *Little Women*, who dies after an illness, was based on Louisa's sister, Elizabeth.

Three years later, the outbreak of the Civil War found Louisa frustrated because women were not allowed to join the army. "As I can't fight," she wrote to a friend, "I will content myself with working with those who can."

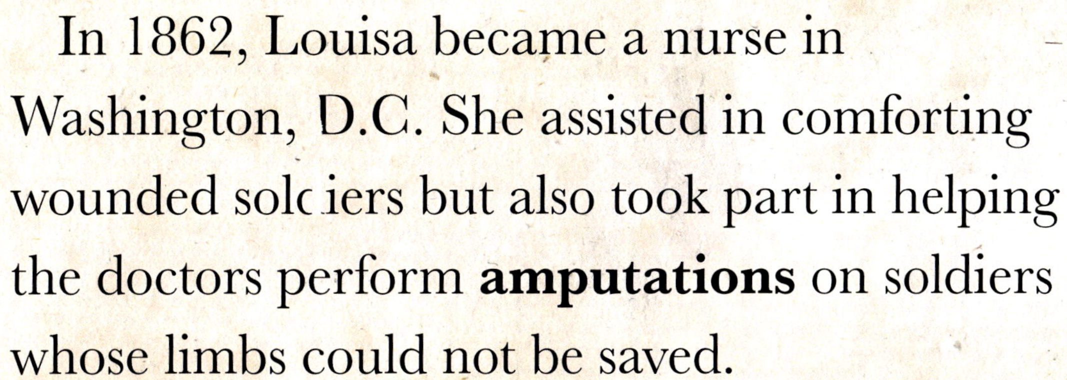

In 1862, Louisa became a nurse in Washington, D.C. She assisted in comforting wounded soldiers but also took part in helping the doctors perform **amputations** on soldiers whose limbs could not be saved.

Unfortunately, after only six weeks, she became seriously ill with **typhoid** fever and had to be rushed home to recover.

Fun Facts

Another woman who worked as a nurse in the Civil War and later became famous was Clara Barton.

Publishing Progress

While working as a nurse, Louisa had written letters home about her experiences. She later used them to create a new book called *Hospital Sketches*. It was published in 1863. The main character, whose imposing name was Tribulation Periwinkle, becomes a nurse tending to the wounded Civil War soldiers. Not surprisingly, her adventures closely echoed the real-life events Louisa had seen for herself.

Louisa May Alcott
1863

Fun Facts

Only men were employed as nurses until the outbreak of the Civil War in 1861.

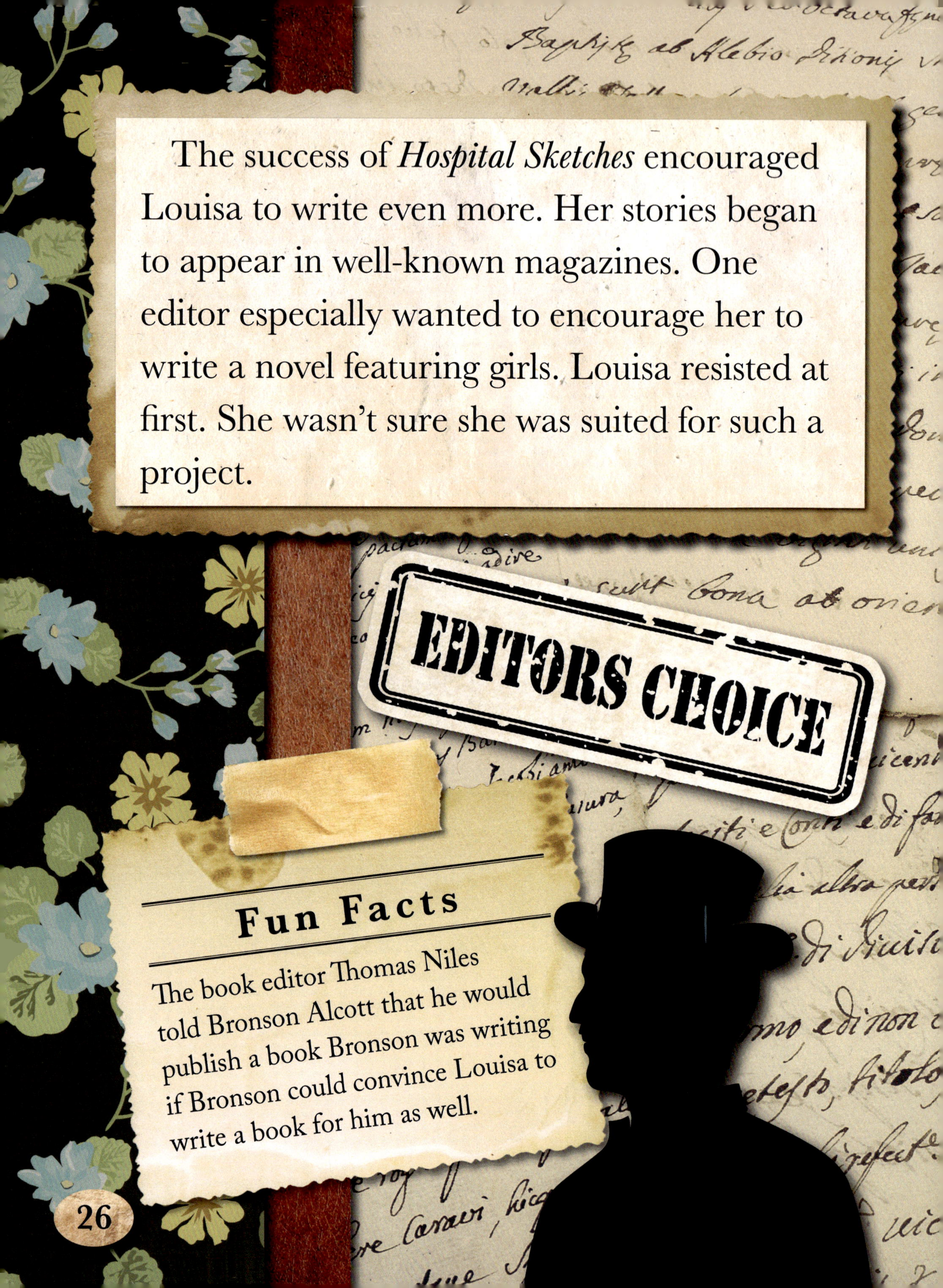

The success of *Hospital Sketches* encouraged Louisa to write even more. Her stories began to appear in well-known magazines. One editor especially wanted to encourage her to write a novel featuring girls. Louisa resisted at first. She wasn't sure she was suited for such a project.

Fun Facts

The book editor Thomas Niles told Bronson Alcott that he would publish a book Bronson was writing if Bronson could convince Louisa to write a book for him as well.

But with the need for money still pressing, Louisa agreed to give it a try. The story centered on the four March sisters — Meg, Jo, Beth, and Amy — and the daily ups and downs of their life in Concord, Massachusetts. It was a story Louisa knew well.

SISTERS

The result, published in 1868, was called *Little Women*. Much to Louisa's surprise, it was an immediate success. Part way through the story, Jo March, the heroine of the book, declares her intentions.

"I want to do something splendid..." Jo boldly informs her family, "something heroic or wonderful that won't be forgotten after I'm dead. I don't know what, but I'm on the watch for it and mean to astonish you all someday."

Clearly, Louisa was voicing her own hopes through her main character. With the publication of *Little Women*, Louisa May Alcott did truly create "something splendid," something that has been read and enjoyed ever since.

Fun Facts

Louisa wrote *Little Women* in less than three months.

Louisa May Alcott was born in Philadelphia in 1832. Her family moved to Boston when she was two years old. Although she worked in a variety of jobs while growing up, becoming a writer was an early dream that she finally saw fulfilled.

After her success with Little Women, *Louisa wrote several more books about the March family, including* Little Men *and* Jo's Boys. *She never married or had children, but at forty-seven, her 10-month-old niece, Lulu, came to live with her after the death of Lulu's mother, May.*

Louisa once wrote, "Nothing is impossible to a determined woman." In her case she certainly proved this to be true. However, despite her eventual fame and fortune, she never was completely free of her family's complicated needs. On March 6, 1888, only two days after her father's death, Louisa May Alcott died of a stroke when she was fifty-five years old.

GLOSSARY

amputations
Cutting off limbs following a severe injury

escapees
People who have left a place where they were held against their will

governess
A woman hired to teach children in their home

naturalist
A student of or expert in nature and natural history

scarlet fever
A disease that causes fever and a reddish rash on the skin

seamstress
A woman who sews and earns money for her work

spirited
Full of energy and enthusiasm

typhoid
A disease marked by fever, stomach discomfort, and red spots on the skin

unbridled
Uncontrolled or wild

Underground Railroad
A secret network of people who helped people escaping slavery in the American South to reach free states and Canada

volunteered
Offered to help out without being paid

INDEX

COMPREHENSION QUESTIONS

What is the name of Louisa May Alcott's father?

Where did Louisa May Alcott serve as a nurse?

How many March sisters did Louisa write about?

ABOUT THE AUTHOR

Stephen Krensky is the award-winning author of more than 150 fiction and nonfiction books for children. He and his wife Joan live in Lexington, Massachusetts, and he happily spends as much time as possible with his grown children and not-so-grown grandchildren.

Written by: Stephen Krensky
Illustrations by: Bobbie Houser
Designed by: Bobbie Houser
Series Development: James Earley
Proofreader: Kathy Middleton
Educational Consultant: Marie Lemke M.Ed.

Photographs:
t = Top, c = Center, b = Bottom, l = Left, r = Right

Alamy: Historic Collection: p. 5 br, 15 tr; Emanuel Tanjala: p. 11 cl; Pictorial Press: p. 12 l, 13 tl; JT Vintage: p. 24 b; North Wind Picture Archives: p. 25 t; Hi-Story: p. 27 r; INTERFOTO/ History: p. 28 br; Granger: p. 6 l, 17 c; Library of Congress: cover bl, p. 29 br; louisamayalcott.org: p. 20 br; Shutterstock: vectorisland: cover tl, p. 22 tr; Naumov S: cover br, p. 8 tr; AVA Bitter: p. 4 bl, 12 br; Africa Studio: p. 5 tr; Arts Studio: p. 5 cl; RYGER: p. 6 tr; Becky Starsmore: p. 7 b; Gustavo Frazao: p. 8 bl; Alexander_P: p. 9 tr; Macrovector: p. 10 tr; hasan02: p. 11 tr; Aleksandr Andreev: p. 13 cr; Mio Buono: p. 13 b; PicItUp: p. 14 tr; quiggyt4: p. 15 c; Jaromond: p. 15 br; DiViArt: p. 16 tr; Zack Frank: p. 16 b; Evikka: p. 17 tl; ArtoPhotoDesigno Studio: p. 18 r; ArtMari: p. 19 tr; BrAt82: p. 19 tr; Photology1971: p. 20 bl; Elena_Medvedeva: p. 22 b, 25 b; Colin Dewar: p. 23 tr; Everett Collection: p. 23 bl; Philphot: p. 24 t; vector punch: p. 24 c; JONGSUK: p. 26 t; Topuria Design: p. 26 b; Ollie The Designer: p. 27 l; Mind Pixell: p. 27 c, 29 tr

---

Crabtree Publishing

crabtreebooks.com 800-387-7650

Printed in Canada/012024/CP20231127

Published in Canada Crabtree Publishing
616 Welland Ave.
St. Catharines, Ontario
L2M 5V6

Published in the United States Crabtree Publishing
347 Fifth Ave
Suite 1402-145
New York, NY 10016

Library and Archives Canada Cataloguing in Publication
Available at Library and Archives Canada

Library of Congress Cataloging-in-Publication Data
Available at the Library of Congress

Hardcover: 978-1-0398-3890-1
Paperback: 978-1-0398-3975-5
Ebook (pdf): 978-1-0398-4050-8
Epub: 978-1-0398-4122-2